Dedications

To all the long and short ears that have brought so much joy into our lives and to the creators of Facebook who have enabled all the friends of these creatures to share their passion.

Special Dedication and thanks to my beautiful JO who has been my guiding light since 2004. Without you, JO, this book and all the 4 legged short and long ears may never have been part of my life.

Eee-ka's True Family

Written by
Bari C. Fischer

Illustrated by
Kathy Pogan

"Why are you crying?"

"I want my mom!"

"Little One - who are you?"

"My name is EEE-Ka. Who are you?"

"I'm JO."

"But where is my Mom?"

"Your mom has had to say good bye to join the donkeys in the sky. She asked me to watch over you."

"I will take care of you now and be your Mama. You can call me Mama JO."

"BUT Mama JO, where are we going? I don't want to leave!"

"My EEE-Ka, we must! We are traveling to a very special place. It has the most beautiful fields where we can run and play, and the grass is lush and green and tastes like honey.

Others like us will be there, and we will have lots of friends. Sleep Little One, and we will be there when the sun rises."

The sun came streaming through the windows.
BUMP, the trailer came to a stop.

"Oh, NO! are we here?"

"Yes, we are - stay close, Little One."

"I'm scared, Mama JO! Who are all these animals?"

"HEEE HAW, HEE HAW

NEIGH, NEIGH, NEIGH

Who are YOU?" they all said in unison.

"I am Mama JO and this is my little one, EEE-KA."

"She is YOURS!"
The donkeys HEEHAWED with laughter.
"Your Little One!"

The donkeys looked at EEE-KA and went "HEEHAW - HEEHAW- you are like us- we make the same sound! How can Mama JO be your mom - she says NEIGH?"

"She's my Mom", HEEHAWED, EEE-KA.

Mama JO neighed firmly, "EEE-KA'S MY Little One!"

The mini horses NEIGHED with amusement.

"YOU'RE the MOTHER? How can you be the mother when you have a long flowing mane and tail, and EEE-KA's mane stands up like a paint brush, and her tail looks like a worn toothbrush?"

The giant black horse galloped up and neighed, "Mama JO, your Little One has giant ears, and yours are small like mine! We all wonder how can how you can be Mama and EEE-Ka can be your Little One?"

EEE-KA turned her head and looked up at Mama JO with giant tears streaming down.

"EEE-KA, looks and sounds do not make a parent and child. Love and commitment do!"

"Every time I look down at you and see that beautiful black cross on your back, I know that I am blessed to have you as my Little One."

"Mama JO when I look up at you and see those beautiful brown hearts on each side of you - I will know that you love me and I love you."

"EEE-KA, you are unique and perfect, you are MINE and I am yours... you are one of a kind, and I will love you and take care of you forever!"

EEE-Ka started HEEHAWING, running and kicking up her heals with joy, calling to all the others.

"I am unique, I am perfect, I am one of a kind, and Mama JO is mine!"

"EEE-Ka, you are my TRUE little one"

"Mama JO, you are my TRUE Mama!"

EEE-KA and Mama Jo flew through the fields jumping, neighing, and heehawing with delight!

The donkeys, mini horses and the big black horse followed galloping with them, kicking up their hooves with happiness and excitement!

"I will love you and take care of you forever!"

When they all stopped running, the big black horse trotted up and whinnied,

"We are all in this together - long ears, short ears, neigh or hew haw, we are here to protect, love, and take care of each other! Big or little, we are one."

"Love has no shape, no color, no sound-just a warm feeling inside of us that glows all the time.

We are here to love, respect and take care of one another. We are a TRUE family!"

The End.

THIS IS A TRUE STORY,
A TRUE FAMILY,
ARNOLD'S RESCUE CENTER.

ABOUT THE AUTHOR & ARTIST

Bari C. Fischer, MED, retired out-patient child and family therapist, mother of 5, volunteer at Arnold's Wildlife Rehabilitation and Rescue Center since 1999, and co-director and co-founder of Arnold's Rescue Center in Brownington, Vermont

Kathy Pogan from Arras, Hauts-de-France, France studied Arts Plastiques at the School of Fine Arts in Douai, France. Kathy's passion for animals, especially long ears, is demonstrated in her magnificent pastels and charcoals of birds and animals. She has become one of the most notable artists of donkeys in France and on the international long-earred sites throughout Facebook.

www.ingramcontent.com/pod-product-compliance
Lightning Source LLC
Chambersburg PA
CBHW042255100526
44589CB00002B/25